marie claire

drinks

acknowledgements

Firstly, I would like to thank Anne Wilson and Catie Ziller for the opportunity to realise a long-term dream and for their continued encouragement and support. Jane Price, my wonderful editor, for sorting out my word salad. Anna Waddington, the most organised gentle woman, who did such a fabulous job co-ordinating this series. The talented Marylouise Brammer for her beautiful design. Lulu, Kathy, Jane and Rebecca for lending their tasting buds and being such knowledgeable sisters in the kitchen. Special thanks to Ben Dearnley, my photographer, and Kristen Anderson, my stylist, whose combined talents speak for themselves in this book. To Michaela Le Compte, who helped me test recipes and did such a magnificent job preparing the drinks for photography. Thanks to Pixie for her divine vodka recipe. And finally a few extra special thank yous... To my friend and mentor, the lady princess Donna Hay, who taught me that anything is possible if you focus, work hard and maintain your sense of humour. To my mum, Matt, Tracey, Paulie, Narelle, Rhearn and Nathan, whose unconditional love allows me to constantly test my boundaries. To Dundee, who always has time to offer the most sensible heartfelt advice. To Birdie and Polly for offering me their gorgeous apartment to enjoy the testing and tasting. To Daz, Annie, Mel, Jude, Nicci, Mel, Michael, Shem and Gabe for being true friends and ever-willing guinea pigs and sounding boards. And, finally, to my dearest most honoured and cherished friend Penel, this is for you. Cheers.

The publisher wishes to thank the following for their generosity in supplying props for the book: Orrefors Kosta Boda; Inne Transform; Funkis Swedish Forms; Plane Tree Farm; White; The Bay Tree; Country Road Australia; Shack; Wheel & Barrow; Papaya; Breville Pty Ltd.

Front cover: champagne berry cocktails, page 20.

marie claire

drinks

jody vassallo

MURDOCH BOOKS®
Sydney • London • Vancouver • New York

contents

simple style — a selection of beautifully
  easy accompaniments … 6
frozen mandarin margaritas … 10
spiced mango lassi … 12
watermelon rosewater slushie … 14
cashew date milk … 16
super indulgent chocoholic shake … 18
champagne berry cocktails … 20
sweet sage, apple and cinnamon
  toddy … 22
peach nectar spider fluff … 24
just-like-grandma-made lemonade … 26
papaya crush with lime sorbet … 28
kiwi apple cider fizz … 30
long tall raspberry and blueberry
  milk ice … 32
cointreau sunsets … 34
creamy rich banana and macadamia
  smoothie … 36
monks spiced mulled wine … 38
melon, pear and peppermint juice … 40
watermelon mint daiquiris … 42
by-the-fire cardamom cocoa … 44

liquorice, spearmint and basil
  wake-me-up … 46
guava juice and soda … 48
apricot and bran breakfast shake … 50
mint daze … 52
tropical fruit frappé … 54
creamy almond and vanilla drink … 56
pinot sangria spritzers … 58
orange citrus crush … 60
raspberry coconut cream shake … 62
cider with midori and floating
  melon bombes … 64
goodness carob, malt and maple
  health drink … 66
packs a punch … 68
pineapple and lychee
  spearmint colada … 70
vitalising beetroot, carrot and
  ginger juice … 72
amaretto liqueur coffee … 74
vodka, ginger and cranberry mule … 76
that's the shot … 78

If you want to team some simple but stylish nibbles with your drinks, try matching up the following ideas...

prunes and garlic wrapped in prosciutto are great with party punch

bake grated parmesan in a hot oven and serve with pinot sangria spritzer

try pear and brie crackers with cleansing watermelon mint daiquiris

enjoy layered tomato, basil and bocconcini with a cointreau sunset

olives and margaritas make ideal table companions

offer some crunchy grissini with guava juice and soda

try deep-fried shavings of sweet potato with papaya lime crush

serve fresh oysters (and a squeeze of lime) with champagne berry cocktails

Serve our sweet drinks with the following simple ideas...

try candied nuts and a couple of glasses of monks spiced mulled wine

dunk rich Greek shortbread in amaretto liqueur coffee

indulge in hand-made chocolates and a chocoholic thickshake

serve toasted pannetone with sweet sage, apple and cinnamon toddies

serve crisp almond bread with creamy almond and vanilla drink

breakfast on grilled apricots and our apricot and bran shake

crunch chocolate-coated coffee beans with by-the-fire cocoa

read your fortune with cookies and a frothy cup of cashew date milk

Originating in China, this tasty citrus was formerly known as the mandarin orange. The weight of the fruit gives a good indication of how much juice it will yield.

frozen mandarin margaritas

1 lime, cut into wedges
salt
ice
60 ml (2 fl oz) tequila
60 ml (2 fl oz) cointreau
2 tablespoons sugar syrup (see note)
80 ml (2¾ fl oz) lime juice
125 ml (4 fl oz) mandarin juice

Run the lime around the rim of each glass. Put the salt on a plate, turn the glasses upside down and press into the salt to coat the rims.
Put the ice, tequila, cointreau, sugar syrup, lime juice and mandarin juice in a blender and mix until smooth and pourable. Carefully pour into the glasses and serve immediately.

Serves 2

To make the sugar syrup, mix 1 cup sugar with 125 ml (4 fl oz) water and stir over low heat to dissolve. Then boil for 5 minutes, or until slightly syrupy. You can also try chilli margaritas: make a standard margarita and add a tablespoon of chilli cordial.

Lassis are popular drinks in India where they are served alongside curries—the yoghurt cools and cleanses the palate. They can also be made with buttermilk.

spiced mango lassi

Put the mangoes, honey, yoghurt, cinnamon, cardamom and milk in a blender and whizz until thick and smooth. Serve immediately.

Serves 2–3

3 ripe mangoes, chilled and chopped
1 teaspoon honey
1 cup plain yoghurt
1 teaspoon ground cinnamon
1/2 teaspoon ground cardamom
250 ml (8 fl oz) milk

Watermelons are now available almost all year round but tend to be sweeter in the warmer months. Choose one that feels heavy for its size.

watermelon rosewater slushie

3 cups chopped watermelon
1 teaspoon rosewater
1 teaspoon lemon juice
500 ml (16 fl oz) lemonade

Put the watermelon in a blender and whizz until smooth. Combine with the rosewater, lemon juice and lemonade and freeze until just solid around the edges. The mixture will freeze more quickly in a metal dish—you need to allow about 2 hours.
Return to the blender and mix until thick and slushy. Serve in tall glasses.

Serves 4

This is a clever caffeine-free alternative to the cappuccino—frothy on top and very very creamy. Don't be tempted to use packet dates.

cashew date milk

Put the cashews and water in a blender and mix until smooth and creamy.
Add the dates and blend to combine. Serve hot, sprinkled with nutmeg.

Serves 2

1 cup raw cashew nuts
500 ml (16 fl oz) boiling water
2 fresh dates, pitted
fresh nutmeg, grated

Chocolate... we all love it, and this is for people who just can't seem to get enough of it. Make sure you use the best-quality ice cream money can buy.

super indulgent chocoholic shake

3 tablespoons chocolate fudge topping
500 ml (16 fl oz) chilled chocolate milk
125 ml (4 fl oz) cream
6 scoops rich chocolate ice cream

Put the chocolate topping, chocolate milk, cream and ice cream in a blender and whizz for several minutes until thick.

Serves 2

A great drink to serve when guests arrive. Make sure the champagne is icy cold. We used blackberries, but you can use whichever berries are in season.

champagne berry cocktails

Put a cube of sugar in each champagne glass and add a dash of bitters to each.
Remove any white pith from the zest and cut into fine shreds (you won't need to do this if you've used a special zester rather than a knife).
Divide the berries among the glasses and fill with the chilled champagne. Serve immediately.

Serves 6

6 sugar cubes
angostura bitters
zest of 1 lime
200 g (6 1/2 oz) fresh berries (blackberries, raspberries, blueberries or strawberries)
750 ml (24 fl oz) champagne, chilled

This is a real winter warmer... apparently British sailors developed a taste for a similar drink in Asia where they used the fermented sap of the palm tree.

sweet sage, apple and cinnamon toddy

4 slices dried apple
2 sage leaves
2 cinnamon sticks
60 ml (2 fl oz) scotch whisky
2 teaspoons honey
boiling water

Put 2 slices of apple into each of 2 glasses or clear mugs. Add a sage leaf and cinnamon stick to each. Add 30 ml (1 fl oz) whisky and a teaspoon of honey to each glass and three-quarters fill each one with boiling water. Serve immediately.

Serves 2

A blast from the past... most of us will remember these from childhood as cola or raspberry spiders. This is a tongue-in-cheek healthier version.

peach nectar spider fluff

Mix the peach nectar and soda in a jug and divide among 4 tall glasses. Float a scoop of ice cream on top of each drink and garnish with a slice of peach. Serve immediately, before the ice cream starts to melt.

Serves 4

600 ml (20 fl oz) peach nectar
600 ml (20 fl oz) soda water
4 scoops vanilla ice cream
1 peach, sliced

An old favourite, real lemonade is making a comeback, and rightly so. If you can get your hands on lemonade fruit, it's perfect for this—you may need less sugar.

just-like-grandma-made lemonade

15 lemons
1 1/2 cups sugar
125 ml (4 fl oz) boiling water
ice
lemon balm leaves
lemon slices

Cut the lemons in half and squeeze out the juice. Put the juice and any pulp in a large non-metallic bowl.
Add the sugar and boiling water and stir until the sugar dissolves.
Add 1.5 litres chilled water and stir well. Transfer to a large jug, add ice cubes and float the lemon balm leaves and slices of lemon on top.

Serves 4–6

There is much confusion about the difference between papaya and pawpaw. We used a red papaya—a small, pear-shaped fruit with red-orange flesh.

papaya crush with lime sorbet

Mix the papaya, lime juice, 2 scoops of lime sorbet and some crushed ice in a blender until thick and smooth. Transfer to 2 tall glasses and float a scoop of sorbet on top of each drink. Garnish with lime zest and serve immediately with spoons.

Serves 2

300 g (10 oz) chopped papaya
1–2 tablespoons lime juice
4 scoops lime sorbet
crushed ice
lime zest

This recipe can be made with alcoholic or non-alcoholic cider. A refreshing drink for a summer's afternoon, it's also surprisingly high in vitamin C.

kiwi apple cider fizz

2 kiwi fruit
juice of 1 lime
750 ml (24 fl oz) sparkling apple cider

Peel the kiwi fruit, slice finely and split between 2 glasses.
Combine the lime juice and apple cider and pour over the kiwi fruit.
Serve immediately.

Serves 2

Any berries are suitable for this drink. When in season, try mulberries. Even those with lactose intolerance can enjoy this drink—it is delicious with rice milk.

long tall raspberry and blueberry milk ice

Chill 2 or 3 long tall glasses in the freezer for 20 minutes before you start. Put the raspberries and blueberries in a blender and mix to a smooth purée. Pour about 1/4 cup of the purée into a jug and carefully swirl in a spiral pattern around the inside of the glasses. Return to the freezer.

Add the milk to the blender and whizz until thick and creamy. Pour into the chilled glasses and serve.

Serves 2–3

Depending on the sweetness of the berries you may want to add a little honey.

200 g (6 1/2 oz) raspberries
200 g (6 1/2 oz) blueberries
500 ml (16 fl oz) chilled milk

drinks

Fond memories of sipping a tequila sunrise on a favourite beach? Here's a new twist on that theme. Use cocktail glasses to keep the layers separate.

cointreau sunsets

crushed ice
120 ml (4 fl oz) cointreau
grenadine
400 ml (13 fl oz) freshly squeezed orange juice
angostura bitters

Fill 4 glasses with ice. Add 30 ml cointreau to each glass, top with a dash of grenadine and fill up carefully with orange juice. Add a dash of bitters, to taste.

Serves 4

The bananas need to be very ripe. If you have some in the fruit bowl, peel and chop them, toss in lemon juice and freeze in an airtight container ready for use.

creamy rich banana and macadamia smoothie

Place the frozen bananas, 60 g (2 oz) of the macadamias, the yoghurt, wheat germ and milk in a blender and whizz for several minutes until thick and creamy. Finely chop the remaining macadamias and put on a plate. Toss the banana halves in the nuts to coat. Stand a banana half in each glass and then pour in the smoothie.

Serves 2

2 bananas, slightly frozen
100 g (3$1/2$ oz) honey-roasted macadamias
2 tablespoons vanilla honey yoghurt
2 tablespoons wheat germ
500 ml (16 fl oz) milk
1 banana, halved lengthways

The secret of a good festive mulled wine is fresh spices and a drinkable wine. We used a Cabernet Merlot which has a soft finish and suits most tastes.

monks spiced mulled wine

12 cloves
1 orange
1/4 cup soft brown sugar
1 fresh nutmeg, grated
3 cinnamon sticks
2 lemons, sliced
750 ml (24 fl oz) dry red wine

Stud the cloves into the orange and place in a large pan. Add the sugar, nutmeg, cinnamon, lemon and 500 ml (16 fl oz) water.
Stir over low heat until the sugar has dissolved. Bring to the boil, reduce the heat and simmer for 15 minutes. Add the red wine and heat through.

Serves 4–6

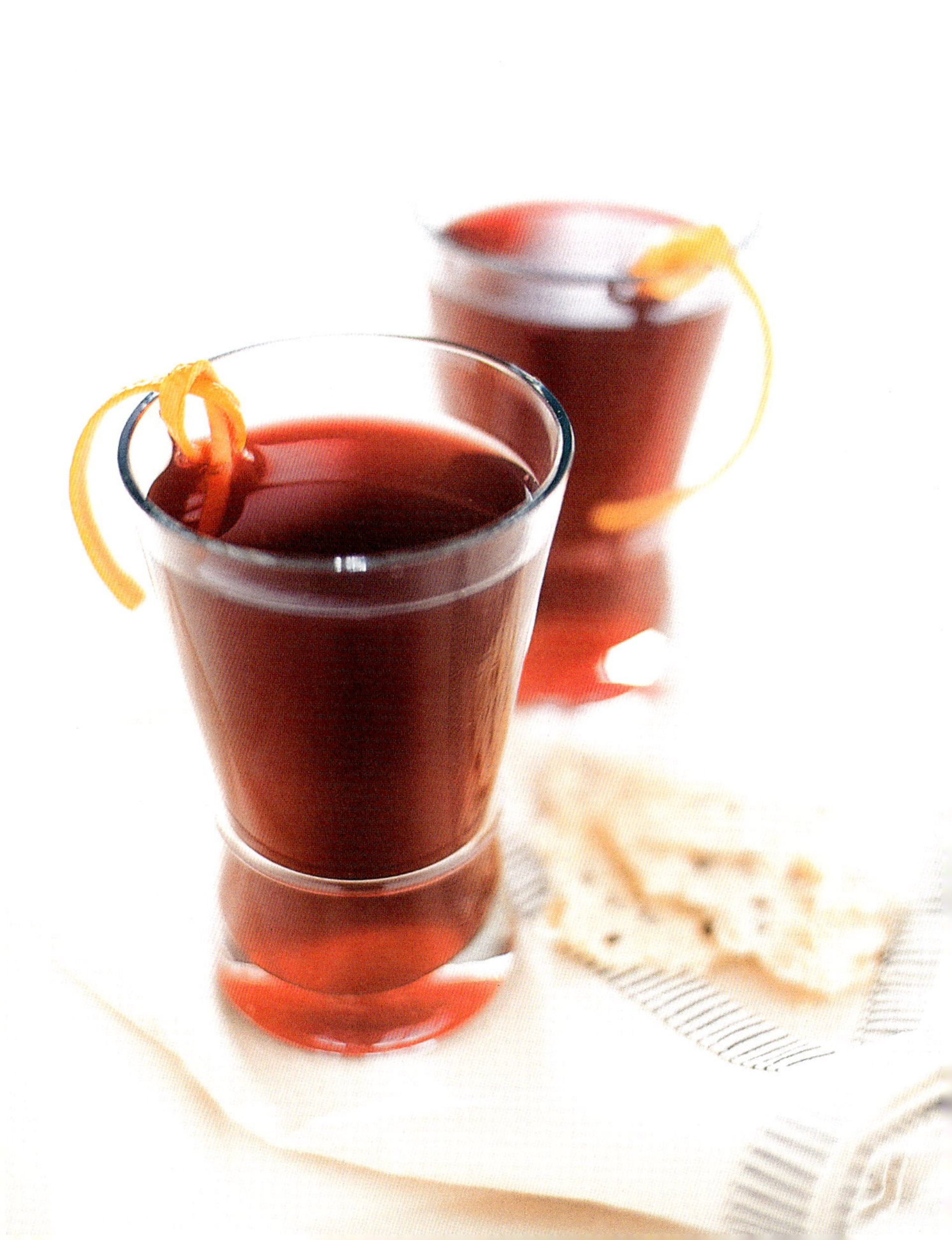

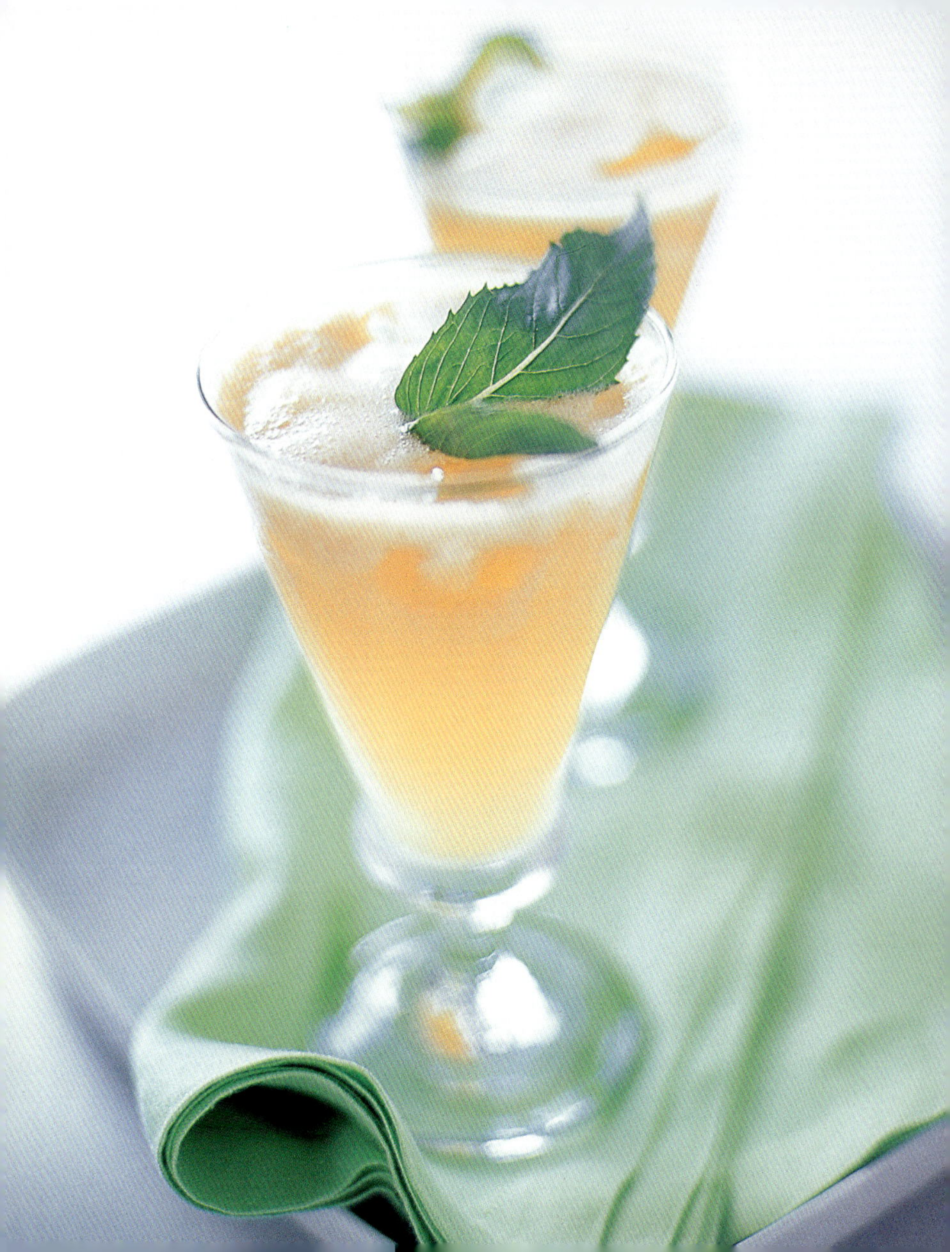

The best way to select a ripe melon is to use your nose... if it has a strong sweet fragrance and thick raised netting you can almost guarantee it's ready to eat.

melon, pear and peppermint juice

Push the melon, pear and peppermint leaves through a fruit juice machine. Serve as is or on ice.

Serves 2

2 cups chopped rockmelon (cantaloupe), chilled
3 pears, chilled, peeled and cored
a few fresh peppermint leaves

drinks

Daiquiris are always popular summer drinks. Use whatever fruit is in season—instead of watermelon, try mangoes, raspberries, pineapple or guava.

watermelon mint daiquiris

ice
120 ml (4 fl oz) white rum
2 tablespoons sugar syrup (see note)
juice of 2 lemons
2 cups chopped watermelon
1 tablespoon chopped fresh mint leaves

Put the ice, rum, sugar syrup, lemon juice, watermelon and mint in a blender and mix until the ice is crushed and the daiquiri is smooth and pourable. Alternatively you can crush the ice, put into glasses, combine the remaining ingredients and pour them over the top.

Serves 2

To make the sugar syrup, mix 1 cup sugar with 125 ml (4 fl oz) water and stir over low heat to dissolve the sugar. Then boil for 5 minutes, or until slightly syrupy. Chill before using.

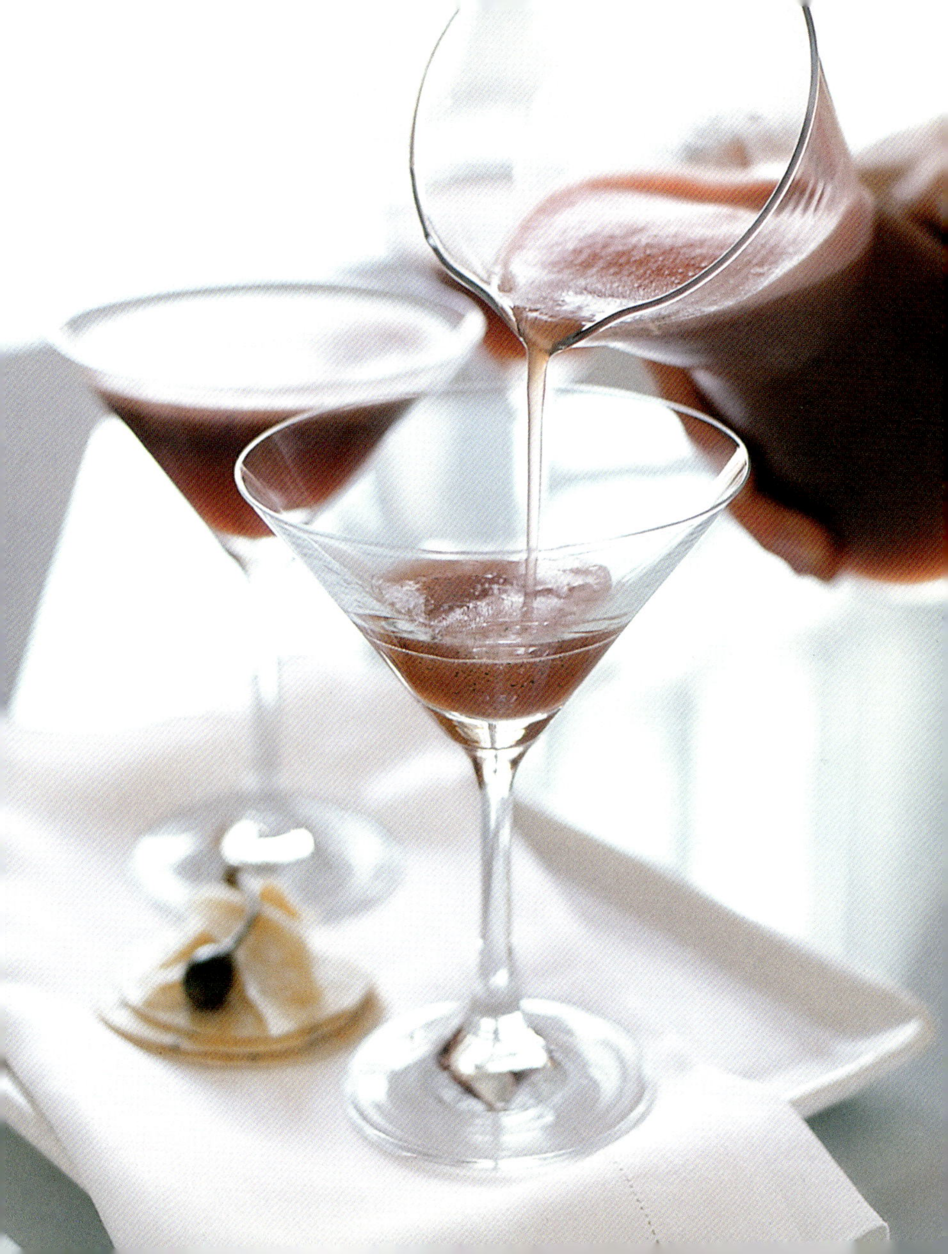

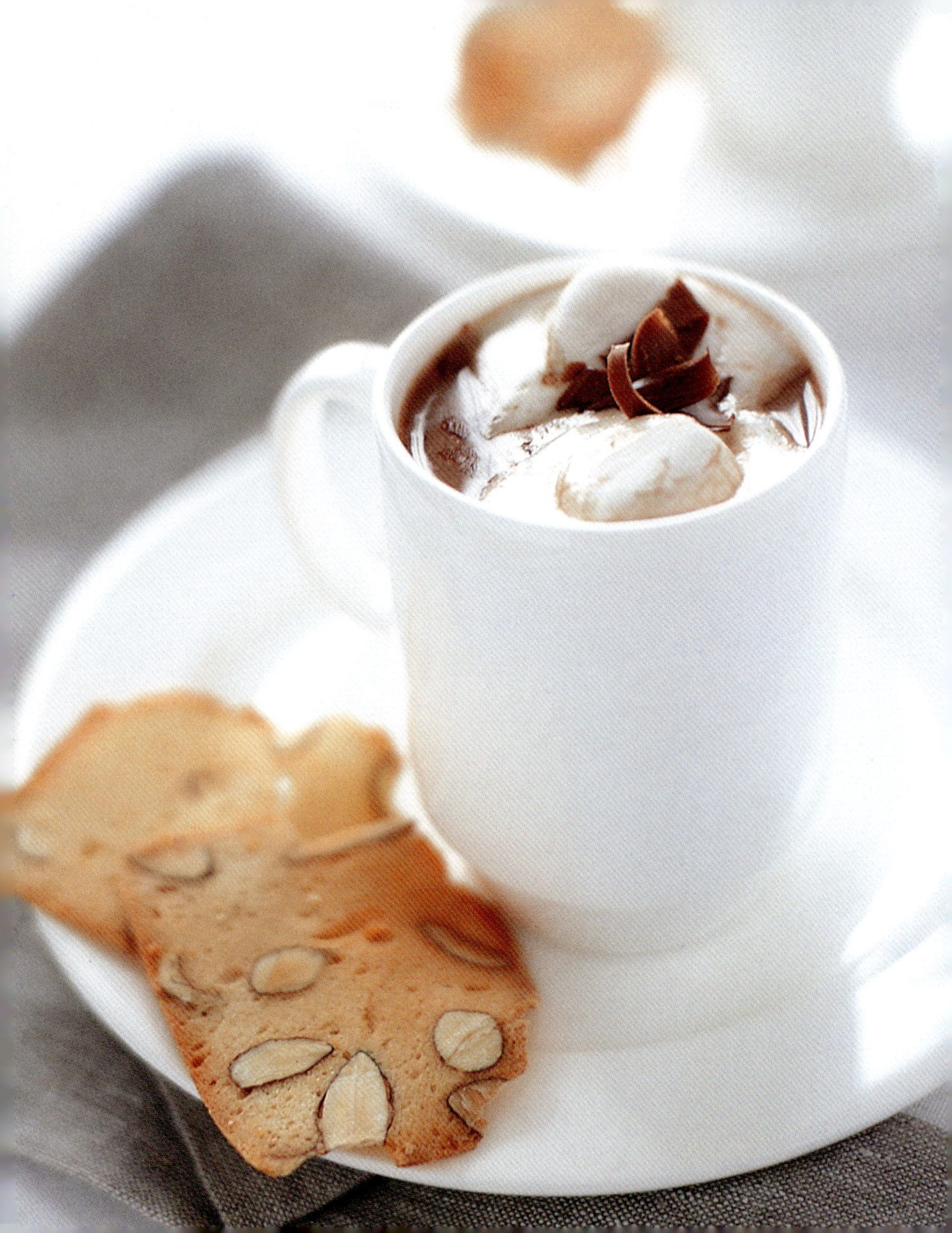

Cardamom is a spice native to India and belongs to the ginger family. A little goes a long way, so use cardamom sparingly. Teamed up with chocolate it's irresistible.

by-the-fire cardamom cocoa with marshmallow islands

Put the cocoa, sugar, cardamom, milk and cream in a pan and stir over low heat until the sugar dissolves. Increase the heat until the mixture is just coming to the boil. Remove from the heat immediately.
Divide between 2 mugs and top with the marshmallows and chocolate.

Serves 2

2 tablespoons cocoa or drinking chocolate
4 tablespoons sugar
1–2 teaspoons ground cardamom
500 ml (16 fl oz) milk
125 ml (4 fl oz) cream
white marshmallows
50 g (1 3/4 oz) milk chocolate shavings

With its combination of sweet aniseed and cooling mint, this tea can be enjoyed hot or cold. The liquorice flavour intensifies when the tea is left to cool.

liquorice, spearmint and basil wake-me-up

1 tablespoon liquorice tea leaves
1 tablespoon spearmint tea leaves
10 fresh basil leaves
boiling water
a few fresh basil leaves

Put the liquorice tea and spearmint tea into a teapot for one. Lightly crush the basil leaves and add them to the pot. Add enough boiling water to fill the pot, put on the lid and leave to brew for 3 minutes.
Strain into a teacup and garnish with some fresh basil leaves. As the tea cools the liquorice flavour becomes stronger and sweeter—add a few slices of lemon if you find it too strong.

Serves 1–2

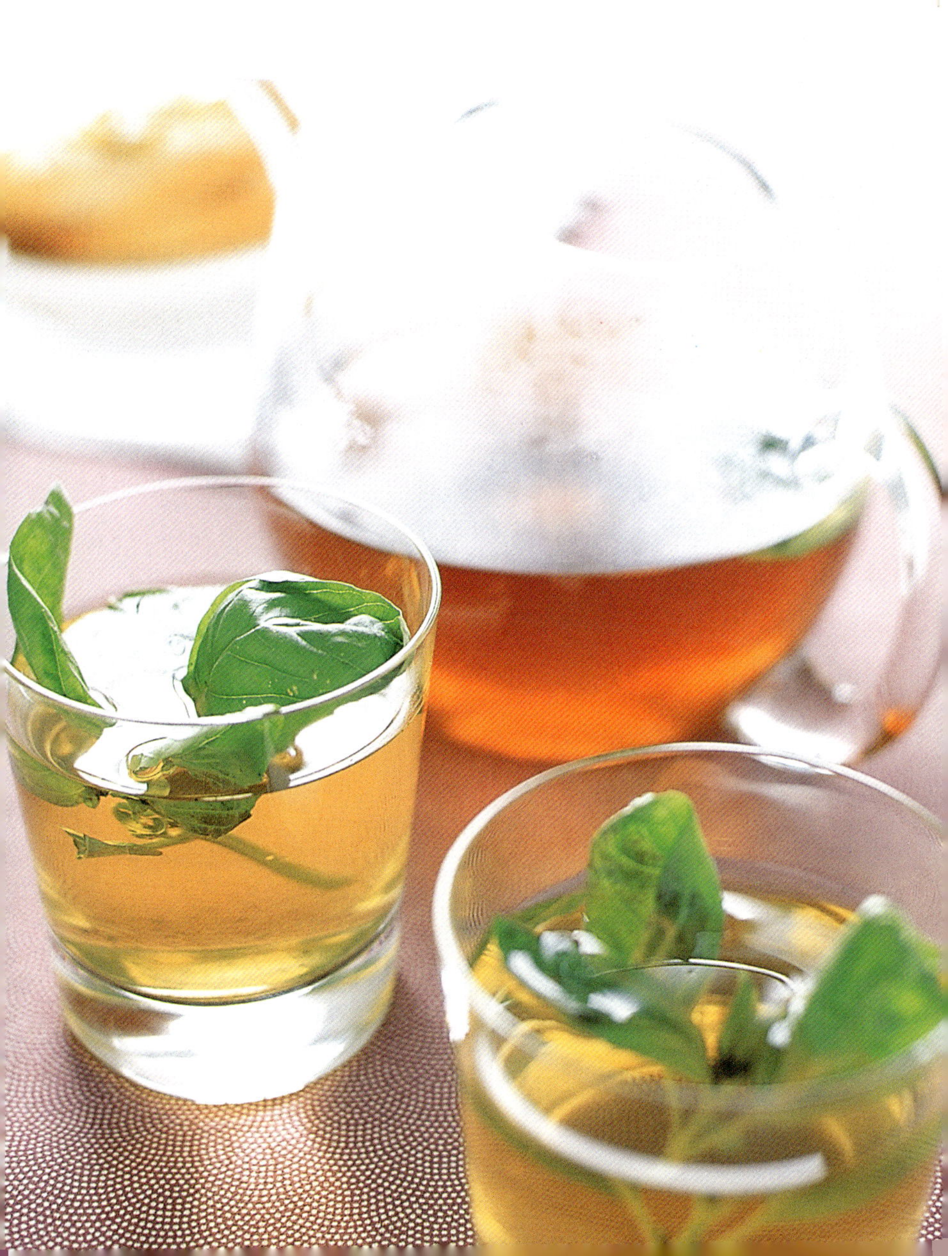

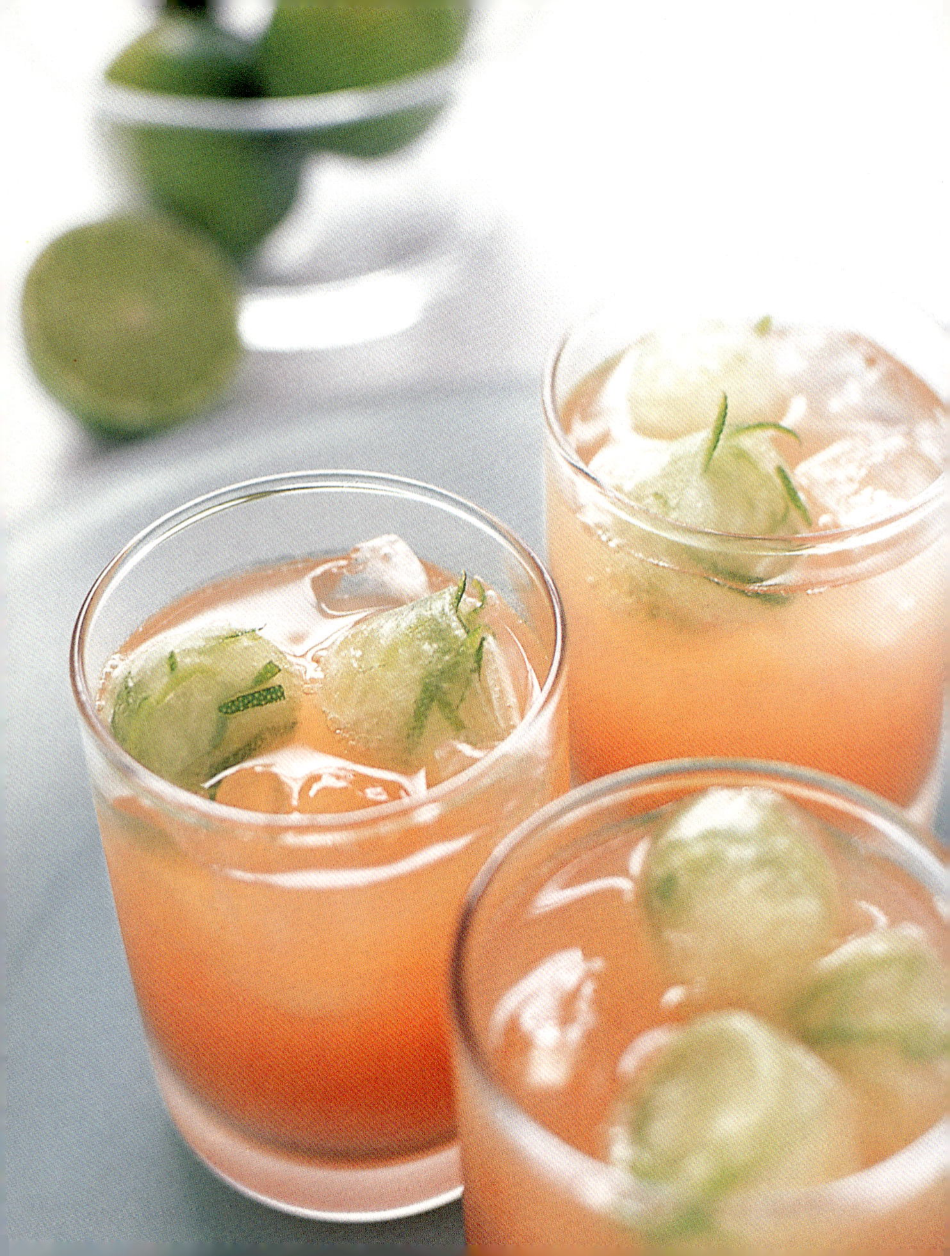

The colour of guava flesh will vary from pale yellow to soft pink. We used pink for this drink as it tends to be sweeter and have a slightly stronger fragrance.

guava juice and soda with zested lime blocks

Put the lime juice, lime cordial and half the soda water into a jug and mix together well.

Pour into an ice-cube tray and top each cube with a little of the lime zest. Freeze until solid.

Divide the ice cubes among 4 glasses and top with the combined guava juice and remaining soda water.

Serves 4

zest and juice of 2 limes
2 tablespoons lime cordial
500 ml (16 fl oz) soda water
750 ml (24 fl oz) guava juice

drinks

What a healthy way to start the day. This drink is high in fibre, carbohydrates and vitamins and, depending on your choice of yoghurt and milk, low in fat.

apricot and bran breakfast shake

100 g (3 1/2 oz) dried apricots
1 tablespoon oat bran
1 tablespoon honey
3 tablespoons apricot yoghurt
600 ml (20 fl oz) milk

Pour enough boiling water over the dried apricots to cover them, then leave until they are plump and rehydrated. Place the apricots, bran, honey, yoghurt and milk in a blender and mix until thick and smooth.

Serves 2–4

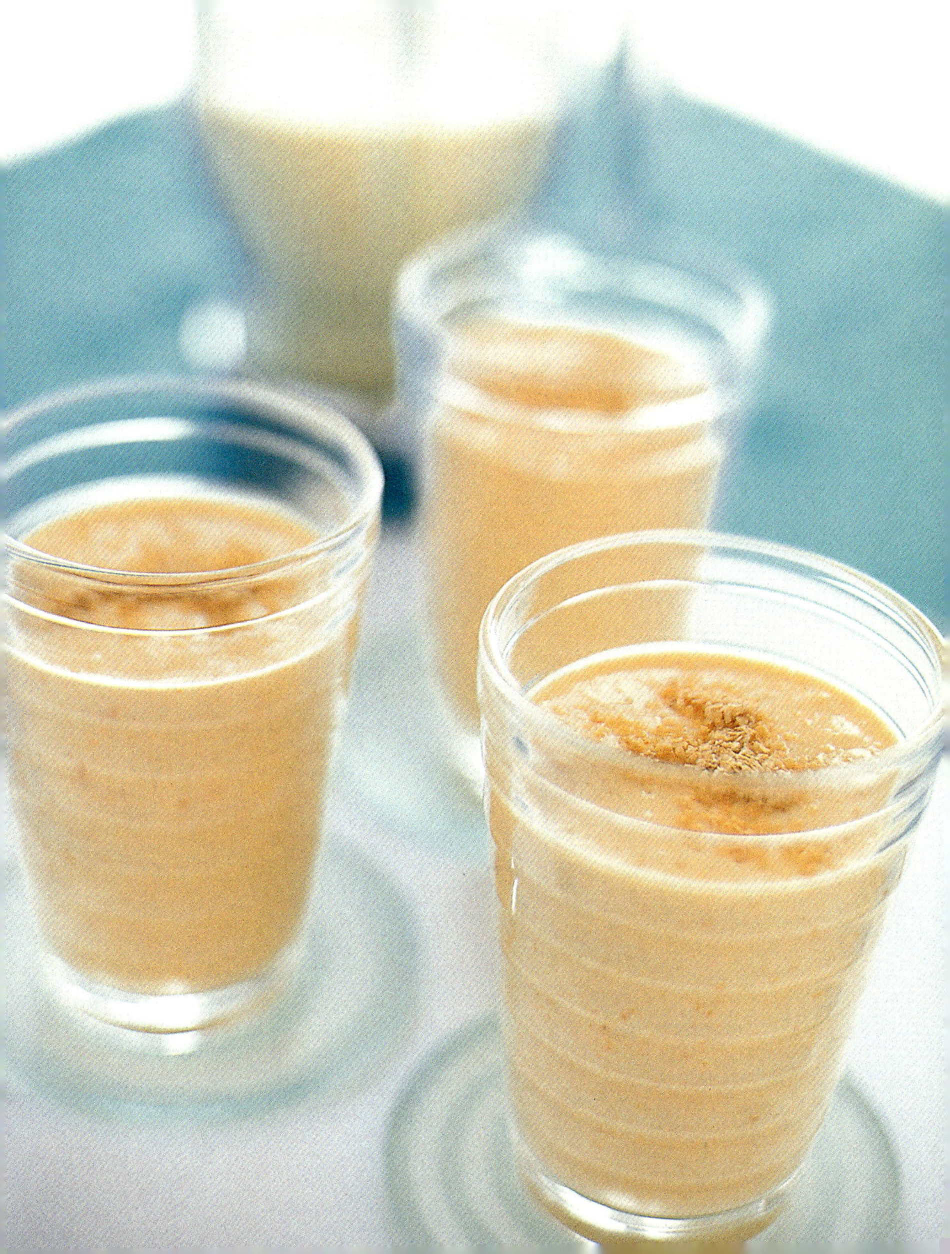

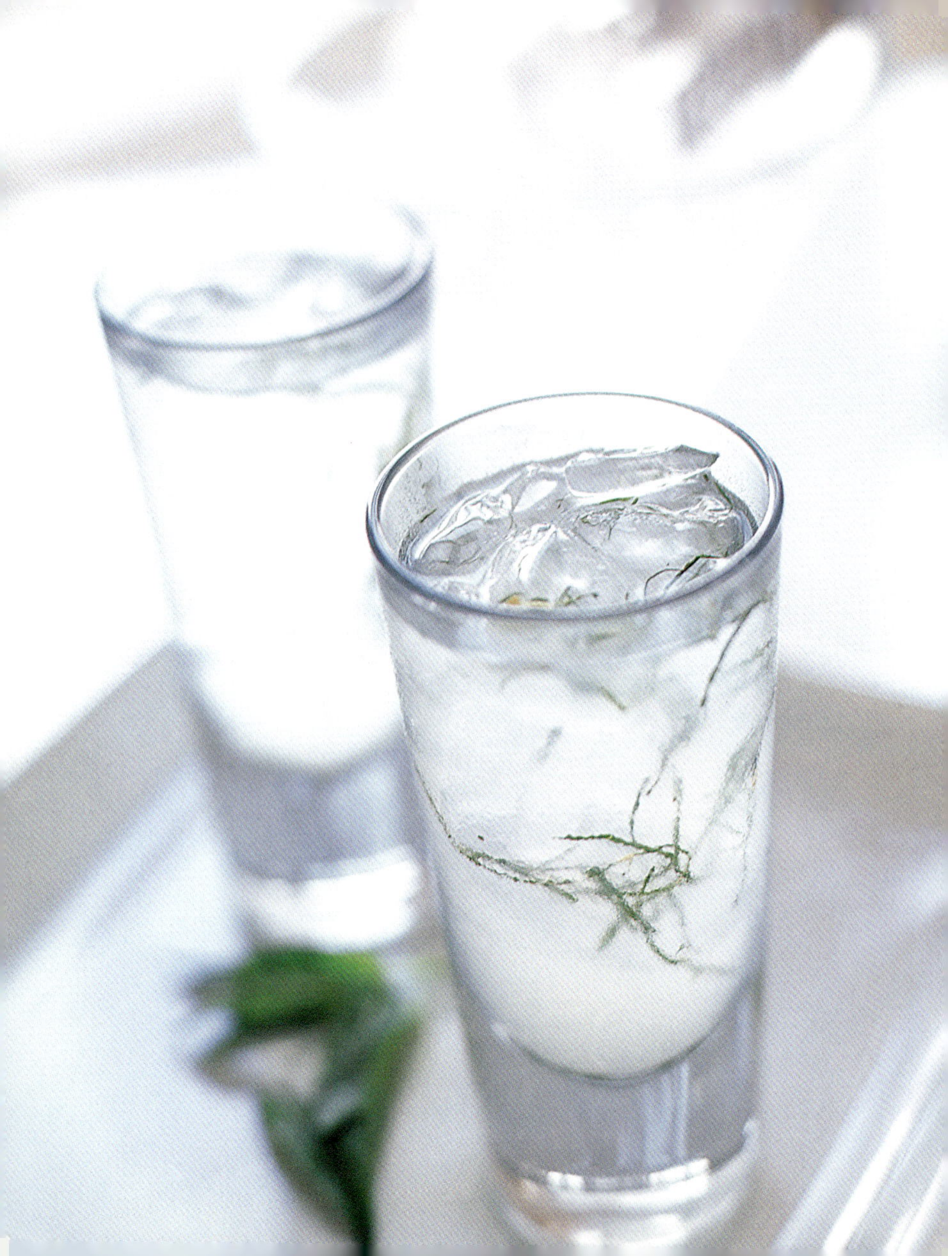

Vodka-lovers beware! This drink packs quite a punch, but you might find it difficult to stop at one. Use fresh-from-the-garden mint if possible.

mint daze

Put the sugar and water in a pan and stir over low heat until melted, then leave to cool.

Mix together the vodka, mint and lime juice and add the sugar syrup to taste. Leave for 5 minutes before serving. Fill the glasses with ice and pour the drink over the top.

You can strain out the mint leaves before serving, but the flavour will be stronger if they are left in.

Serves 2

1/2 cup sugar
3 tablespoons water
80 ml (2 3/4 fl oz) vodka
1/4 cup fresh mint leaves, finely shredded
1–2 tablespoons lime juice
ice

drinks

These drinks make a great breakfast in a glass. The fruit must be ripe or you'll need to add sugar. Add a little coconut milk if you prefer a creamy drink.

tropical fruit frappé

1 cup chopped rockmelon (cantaloupe)
1 banana, chopped
1 cup chopped pawpaw
1 cup chopped pineapple
1 mango, chopped
250 ml (8 fl oz) pineapple juice
crushed ice

Put the melon, banana, pawpaw, pineapple and mango in a blender and whizz until smooth.

Add the pineapple juice and ice and blend until the frappé is thick and the ice has thoroughly broken down.

Serves 4

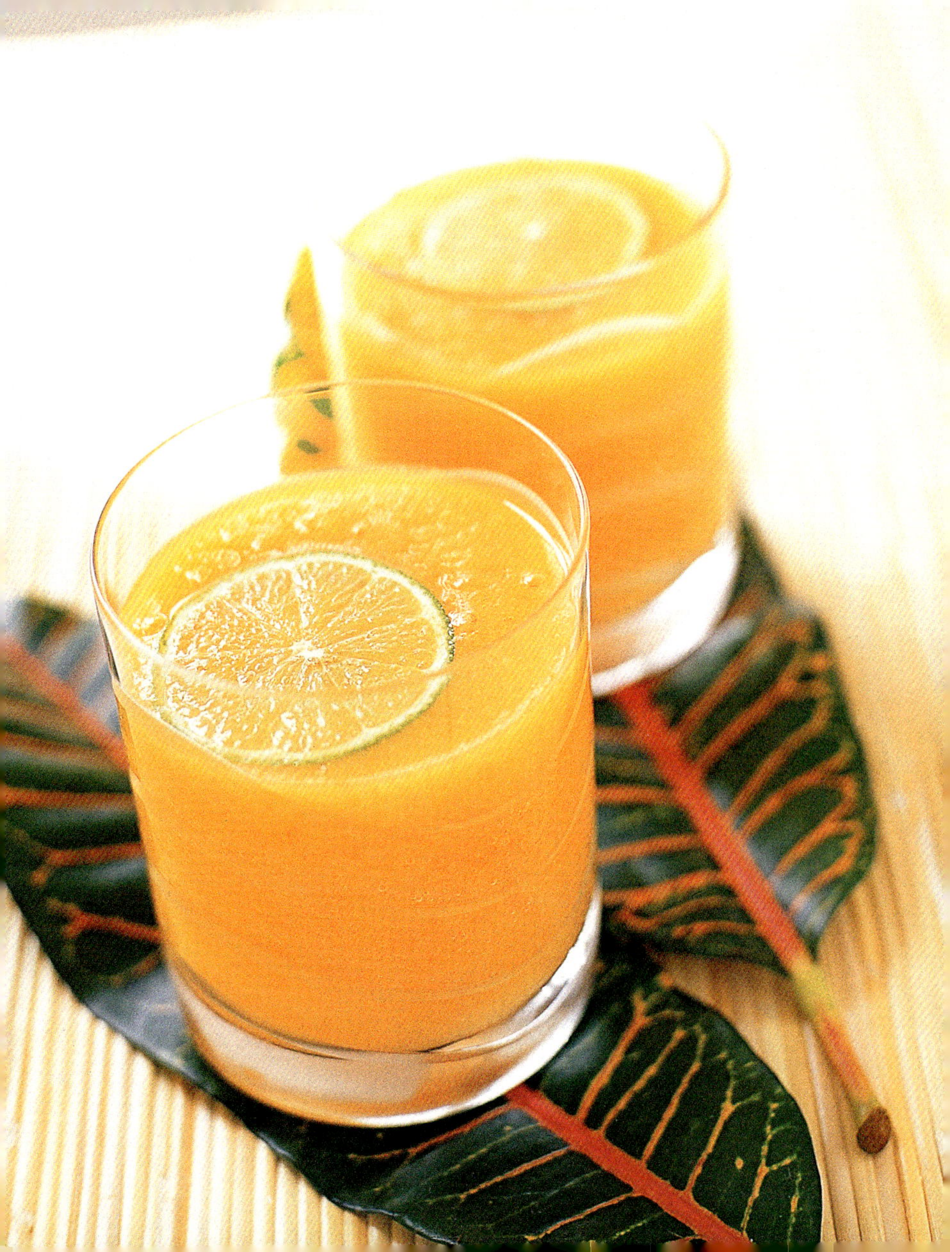

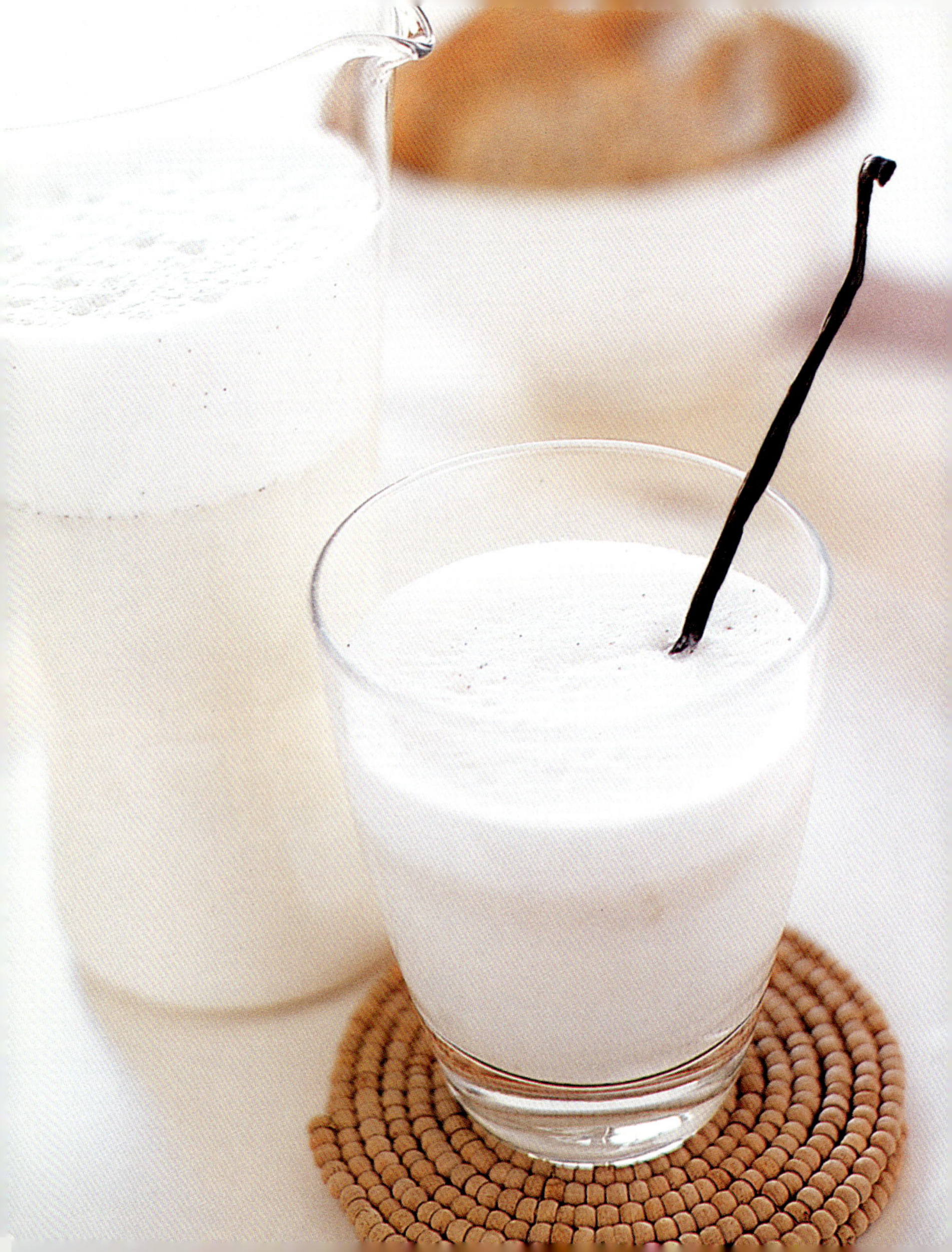

You can rinse the vanilla bean, let it dry and put it in an airtight container of caster sugar. Use this vanilla sugar to flavour the drink in place of the maple syrup.

creamy almond and vanilla drink

Put the vanilla bean and milk in a saucepan and heat until just about to come to the boil. Remove from the heat immediately and then leave to infuse for 5 minutes. Return to the heat and heat again until just about to come to the boil. Remove the vanilla bean. Put the milk, almonds, syrup and almond essence in a blender and whizz until smooth, thick and creamy.

Serves 2

1 vanilla bean, split in half
500 ml (16 fl oz) milk
1/2 cup raw almonds, toasted
1 tablespoon pure maple syrup
1 teaspoon almond essence

Enjoyed by the Spanish for centuries, the name sangria comes from their word for 'blood'. This wonderfully light drink can also be made with white wine.

pinot sangria spritzers

ice
750 ml (24 fl oz) pinot noir
250 ml (8 fl oz) orange juice
1 orange, sliced into half moons
1 lemon, sliced into half moons
1 lime, sliced into half moons
500 ml (16 fl oz) soda water with a hint of lemon or lime

Put the ice, pinot and orange juice in a large jug and stir well.
Add the sliced fruit and leave in the fridge to chill for 30 minutes.
Add the soda water and serve in tall glasses, with extra ice if you like.

Serves 4–6

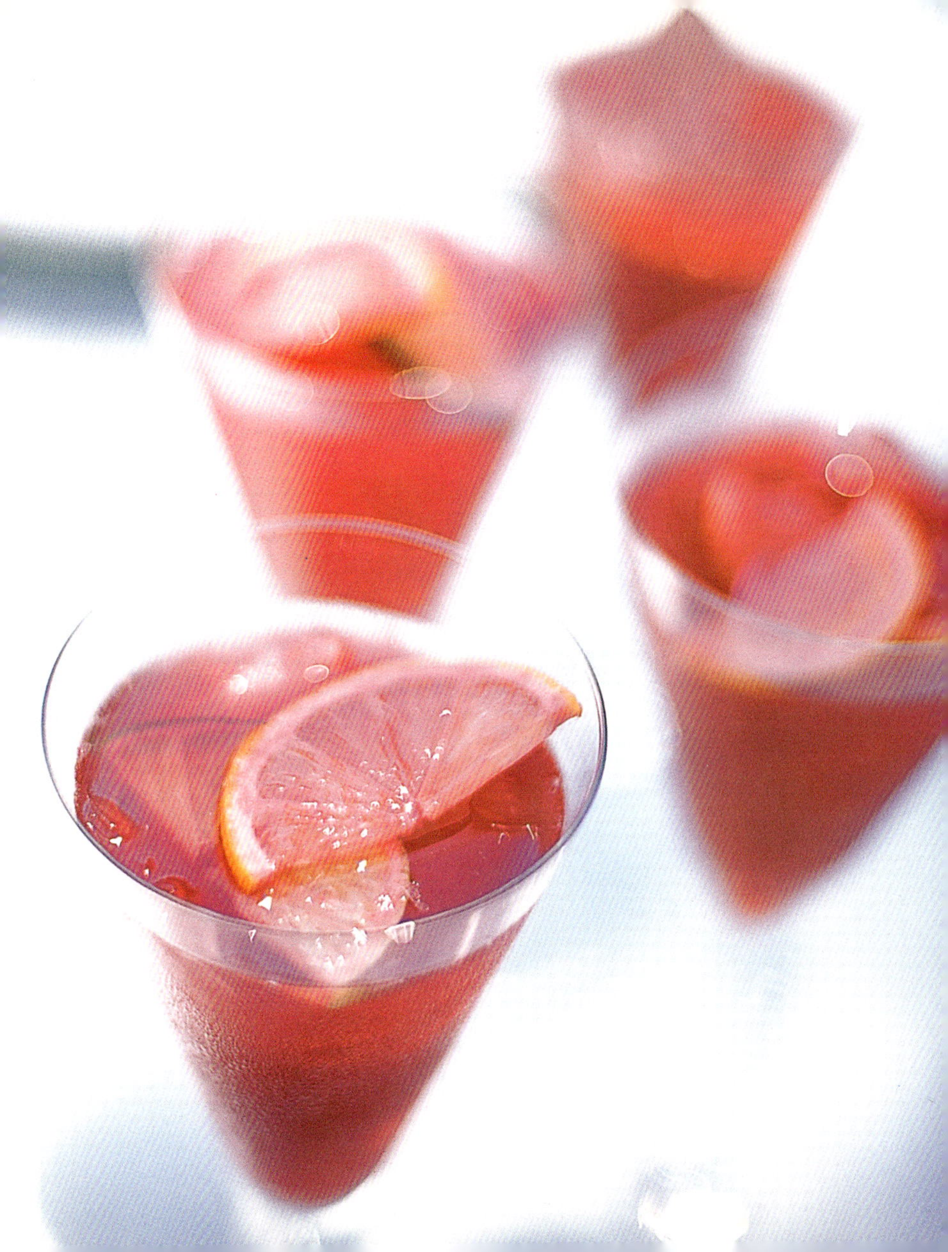

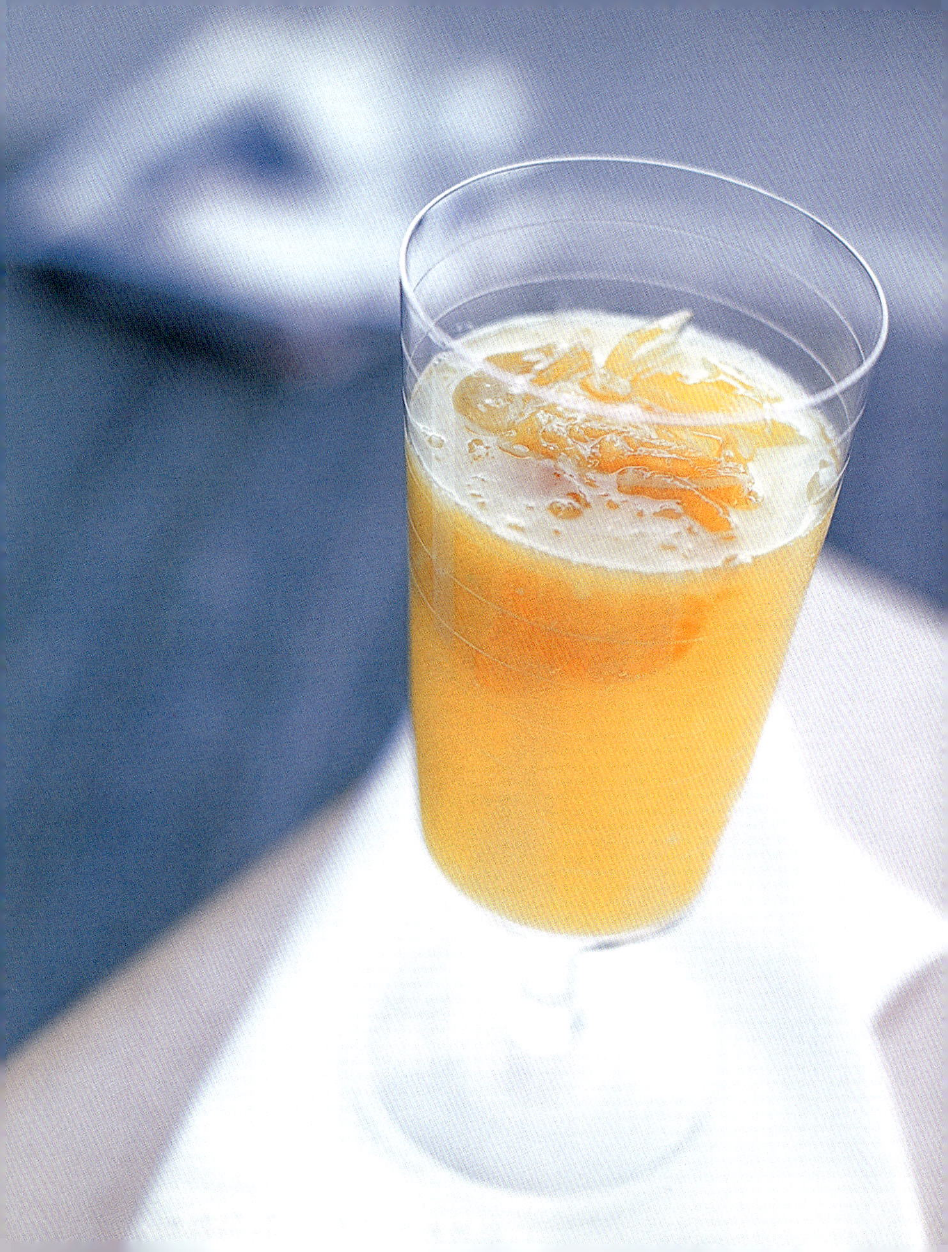

The juice of navel (seedless) oranges needs to be drunk within minutes of juicing the fruit or it will turn bitter. Use blood oranges for this drink, when they're in season.

orange citrus crush

Segment 2 of the oranges and juice the remainder—don't strain the juice, you can keep the pulp in it. Add the lime zest and juice to the orange juice. Add the orange segments and sugar to taste. Stir well and serve over ice.

Serves 4

12 navel oranges
zest and juice of 1 lime
sugar, to taste
ice

Considered the 'queen of berries', the raspberry is packed full of vitamin C. For a low-fat drink, blend with ice instead of coconut cream and ice cream.

raspberry coconut cream shake

200 g (6 1/2 oz) raspberries (fresh or frozen)
250 ml (8 fl oz) apple and blackcurrant juice
400 ml (13 fl oz) coconut cream
2 scoops raspberry ripple ice cream
marshmallows

Put the raspberries, apple and blackcurrant juice, coconut cream and ice cream in a blender and mix for several minutes until thick and creamy. Thread marshmallows onto 4 swizzle sticks and serve with the drinks. You might also like to serve with a straw and a long spoon.

Serves 2–4

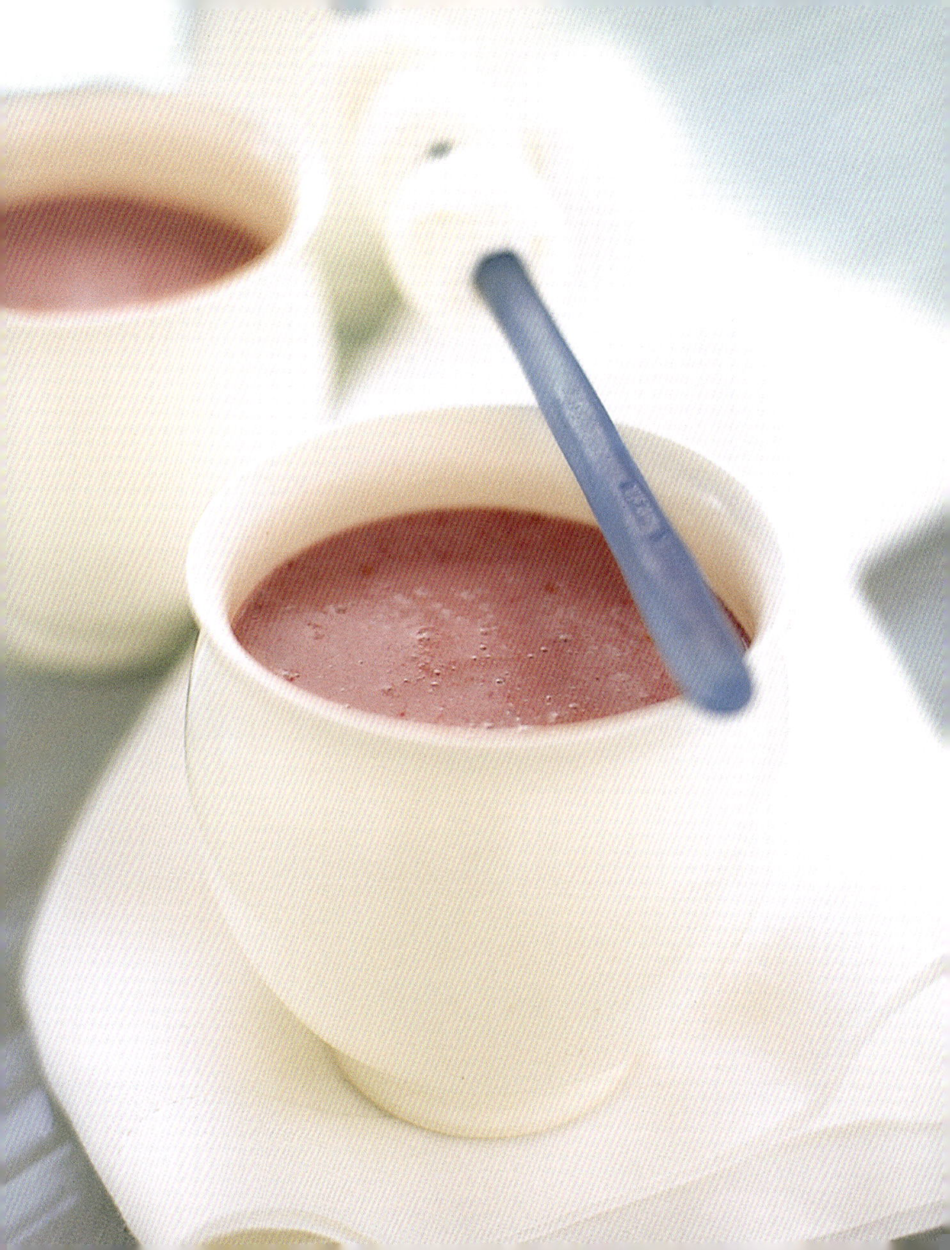

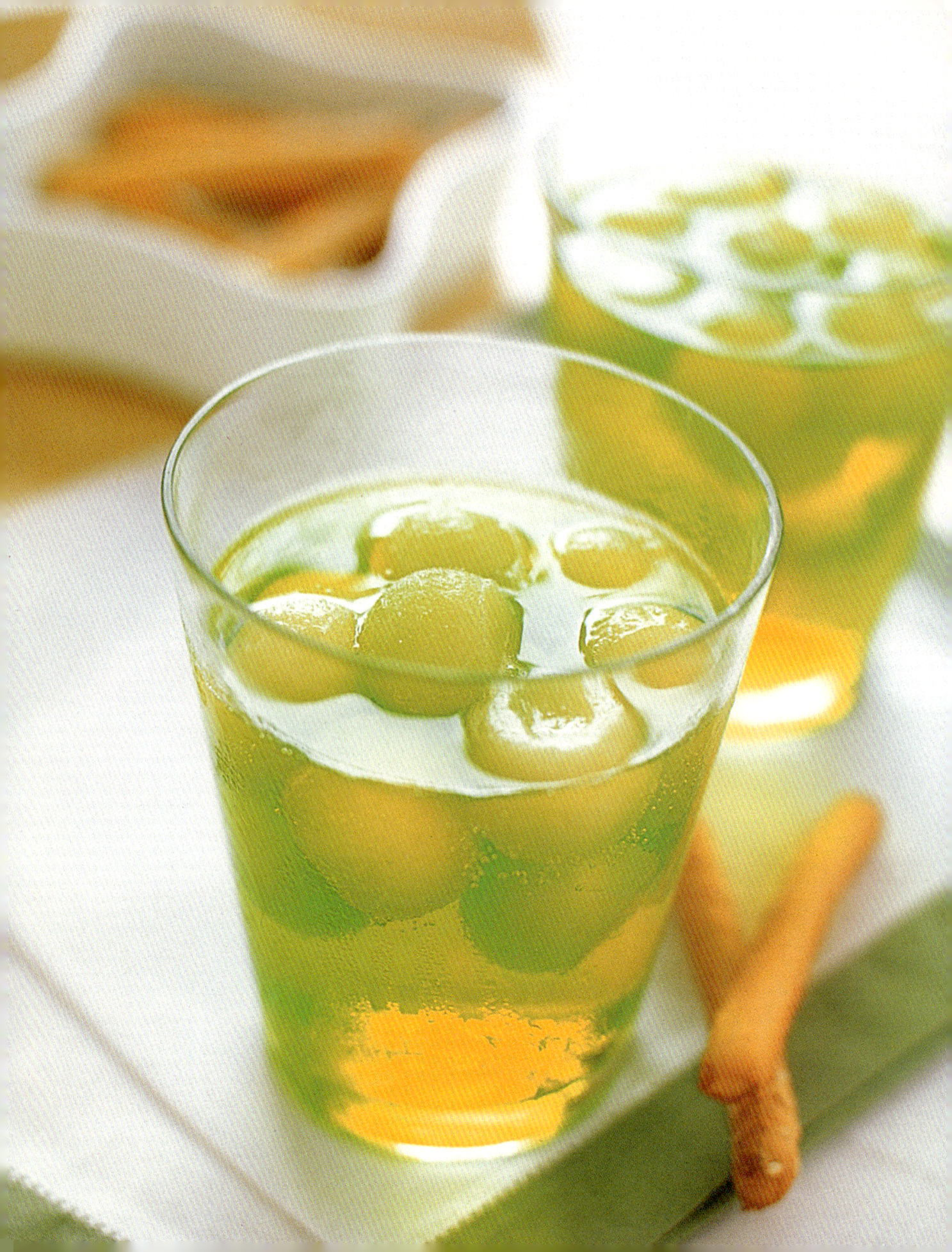

The humble honeydew has been enjoyed for thousands of years. Unlike the watermelon, it will continue to ripen at room temperature after it's been picked.

cider with midori and floating melon bombes

Use a melon baller to scoop out balls of the honeydew melon. Put on a baking tray and freeze until solid. Divide the midori among 4 glasses, then carefully pour in the cider to half fill the glasses. Top with the frozen melon balls.

Serves 4

1 small honeydew melon
185 ml (6 fl oz) midori
750 ml (24 fl oz) alcoholic apple cider, chilled

drinks

With less kilojoules than chocolate and no caffeine, carob is taking off in popularity. You could use cocoa powder instead, but it's not quite as sweet.

goodness carob, malt and maple health drink

1 litre (32 fl oz) vanilla soy milk, chilled
4 tablespoons malt powder
2 tablespoons carob powder
2 tablespoons pure maple syrup

Put the soy milk, malt powder, carob powder and maple syrup in a blender and whizz until thick and creamy.

Serves 4

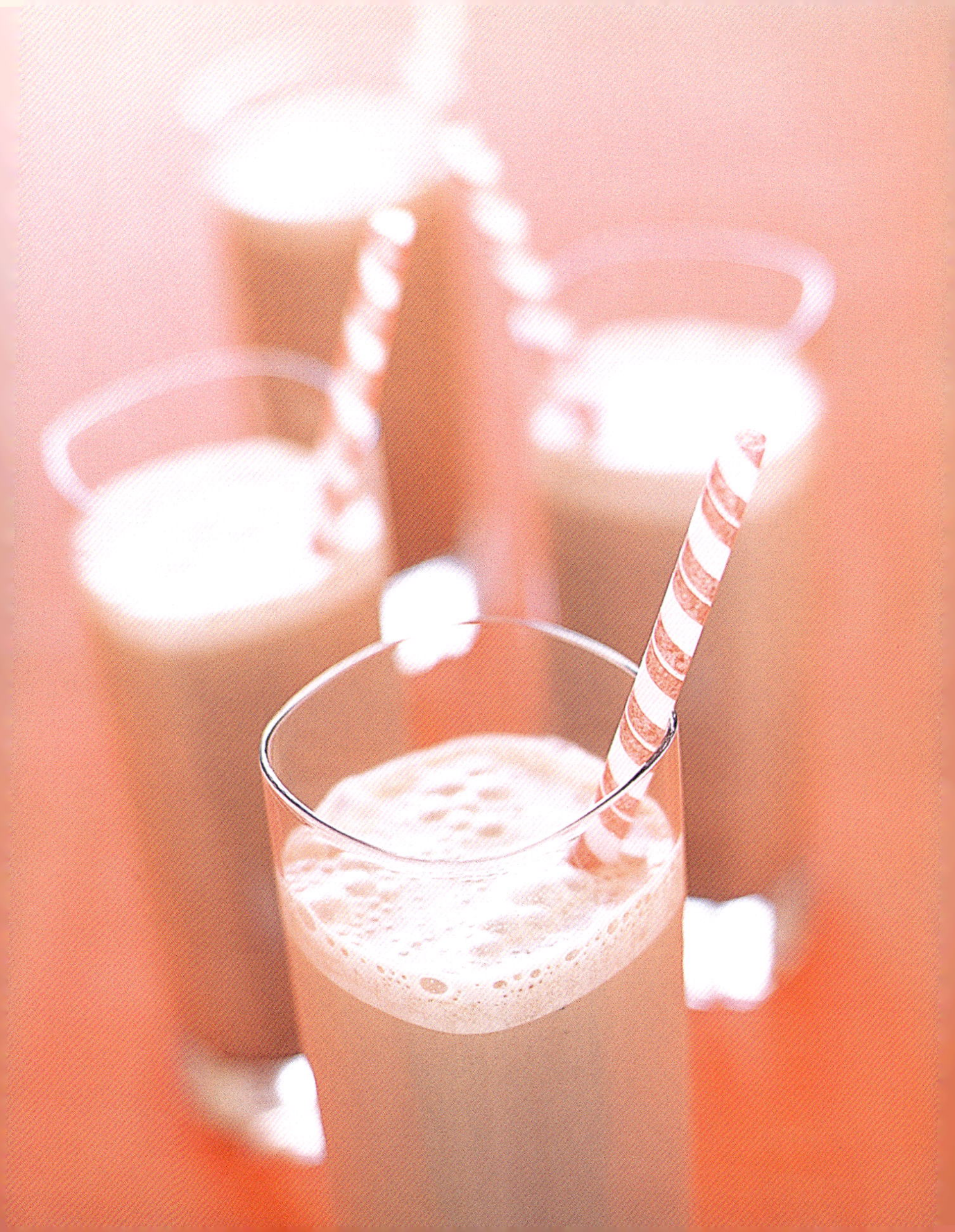

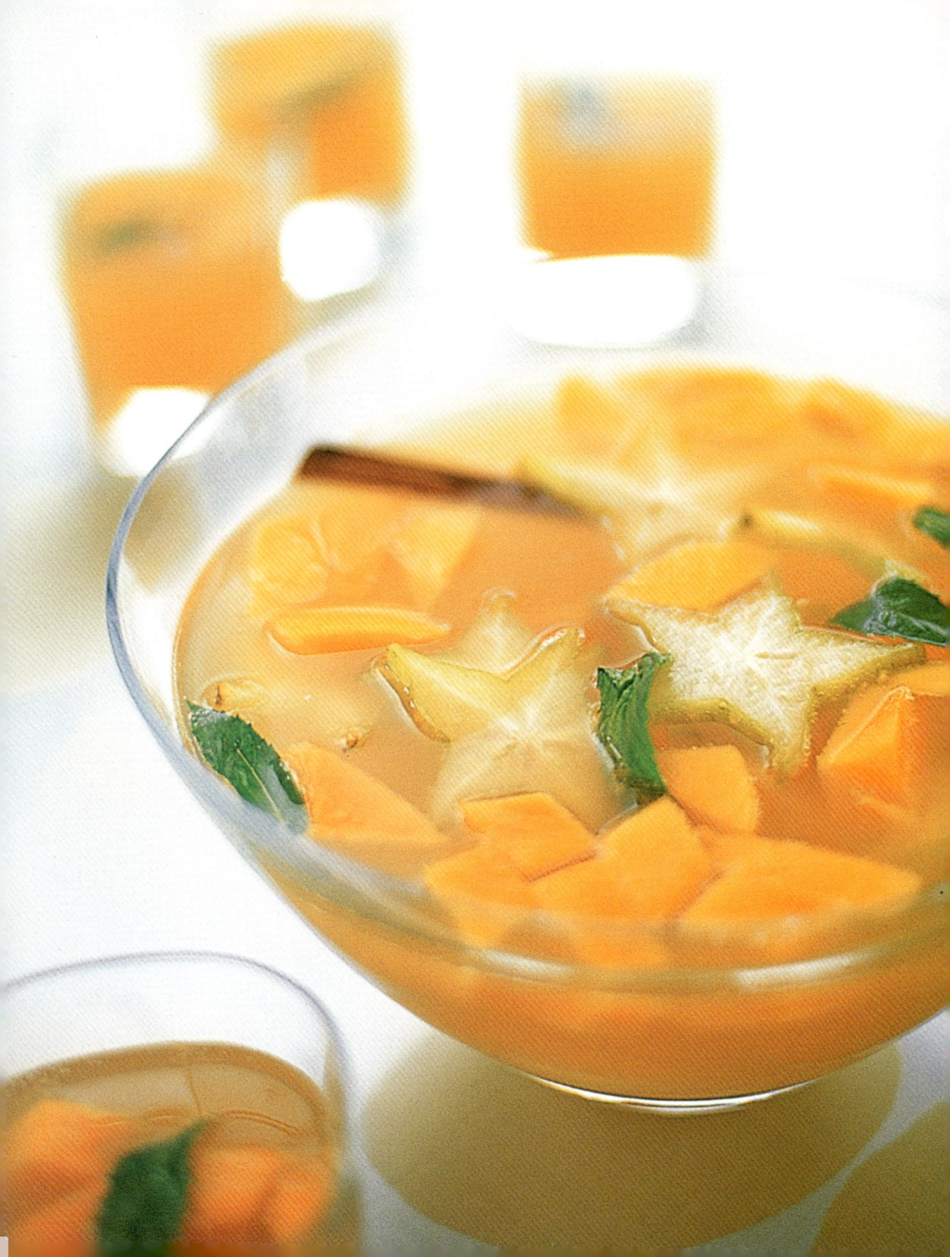

What's a party without punch? We've chosen tropical fruit for our drink, although most fruits are suitable for making punch. Warn your friends... it *is* alcoholic.

packs a punch

Place a block of ice in a large bowl, add the fruit, apple and guava juice, pineapple juice, cinnamon sticks and ginger ale. Leave to chill in the fridge for 30 minutes.
Add the champagne and mint leaves and serve immediately.

Serves 10–15

ice
3 starfruit, sliced
3 mangoes, sliced
1 red papaya, chopped
250 ml (8 fl oz) apple and guava juice
1 litre (32 fl oz) pineapple juice
2 cinnamon sticks
750 ml (24 fl oz) dry ginger ale
2 x 750 ml (24 fl oz) bottles champagne
fresh mint leaves

The lychee is one of China's most cherished fruits and has been so for over 2000 years. As its season is relatively short, we've used canned for this recipe.

pineapple and lychee spearmint colada

750 ml (24 fl oz) pineapple juice
500 g (1 lb) canned lychees
2 tablespoons spearmint leaves (the pointed ones that look like spears)
2 cups chopped pineapple
125 ml (4 fl oz) coconut cream
crushed ice

Put the pineapple juice, lychees and their juice, spearmint and pineapple in a blender and mix until smooth.
Add the coconut cream and ice and blend until thick and smooth.
Serve immediately.

Serves 6–8

You can add a splash of white rum to this drink if you fancy a cocktail.

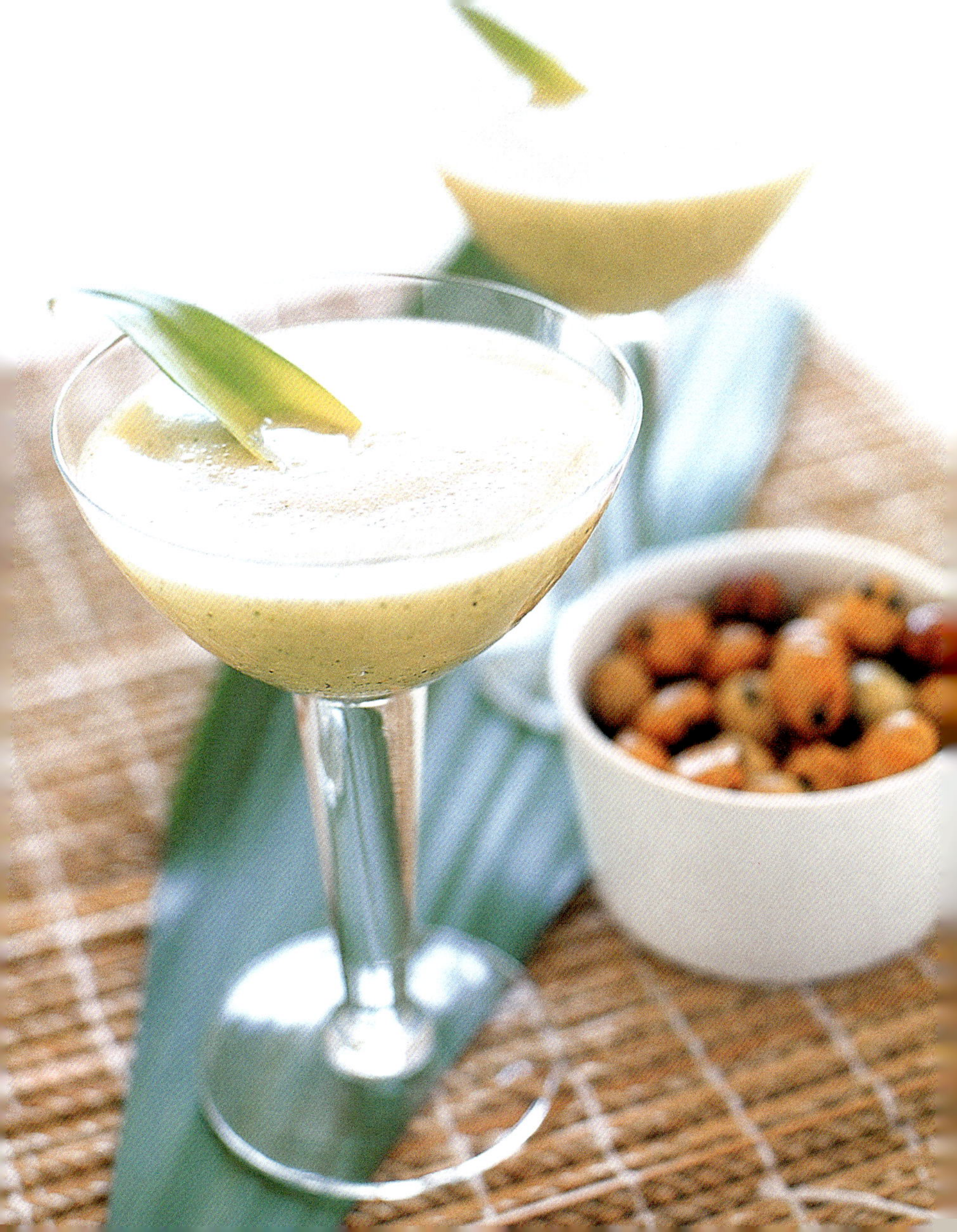

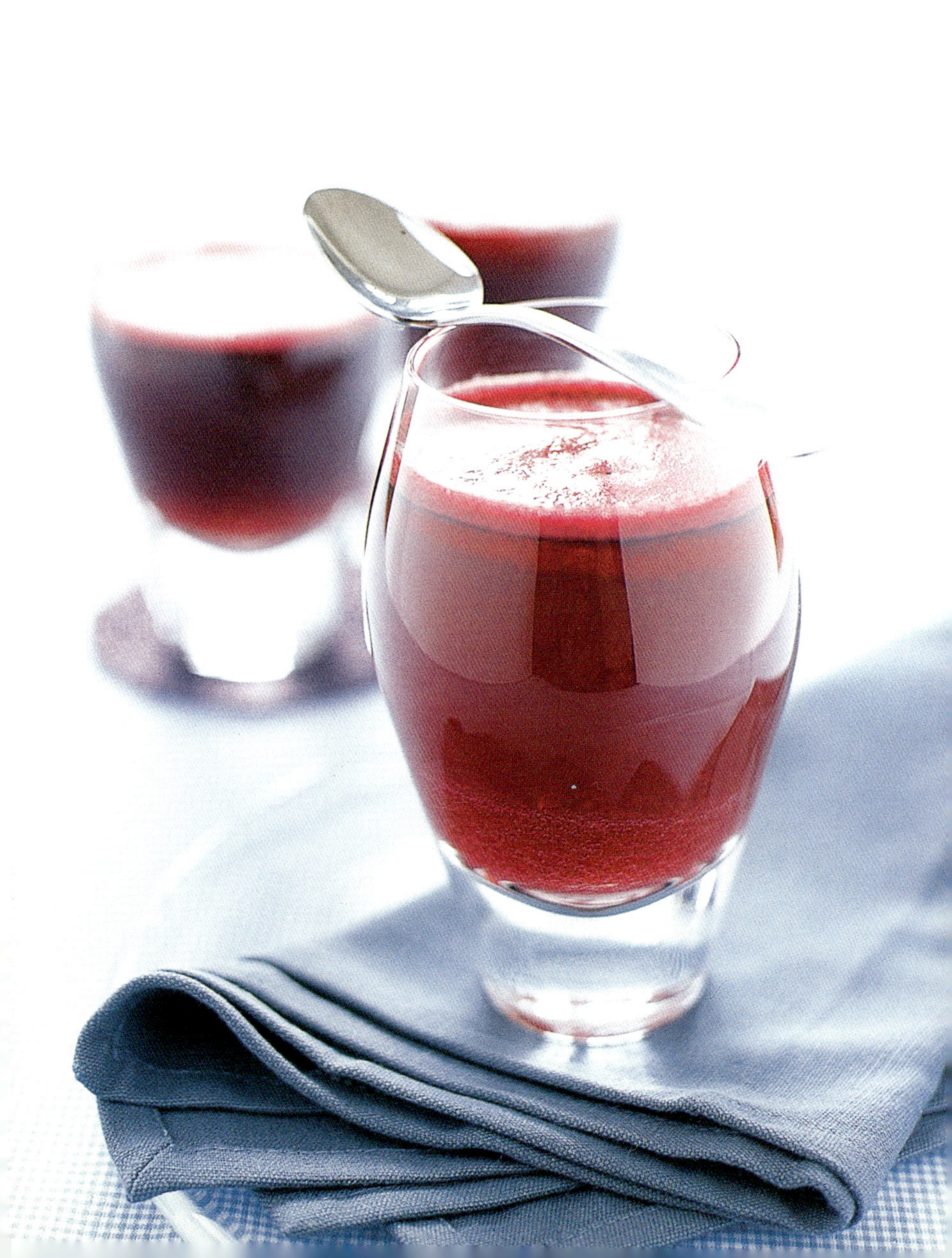

This drink is seriously good for you, but that doesn't mean it has to taste like it. The beetroot and carrot are surprisingly sweet and fresh ginger gives a hint of spice.

vitalising beetroot, carrot and ginger juice

Peel the beetroot, carrot and ginger—wear gloves when you do this to prevent the beetroot staining your hands.
Push the ingredients separately through a juicing machine, then give it a good stir and serve immediately.

Serves 2

1 fresh beetroot bulb
6 carrots
3 cm (1 inch) piece of fresh ginger

It doesn't come much better than this… a luxurious drink featuring all those goodies we try to avoid. A little indulgence is a wonderful thing.

amaretto liqueur coffee

100 g (3 1/2 oz) dark chocolate, melted
60 ml (2 fl oz) amaretto
600 ml (20 fl oz) hot strong espresso coffee
125 ml (4 fl oz) cream
1 tablespoon pure maple syrup
50 g (1 3/4 oz) vienna almonds

Coat 2 spoons with the melted chocolate and leave on a saucer in the fridge to set. Divide the amaretto between 2 coffee glasses. Pour the coffee over the amaretto.
Whisk the cream until stiff peaks form, then fold in the maple syrup. Roughly chop the almonds. Spoon a dollop of cream onto each coffee and sprinkle with the chopped almonds. Serve with the chocolate spoons.

Serves 2

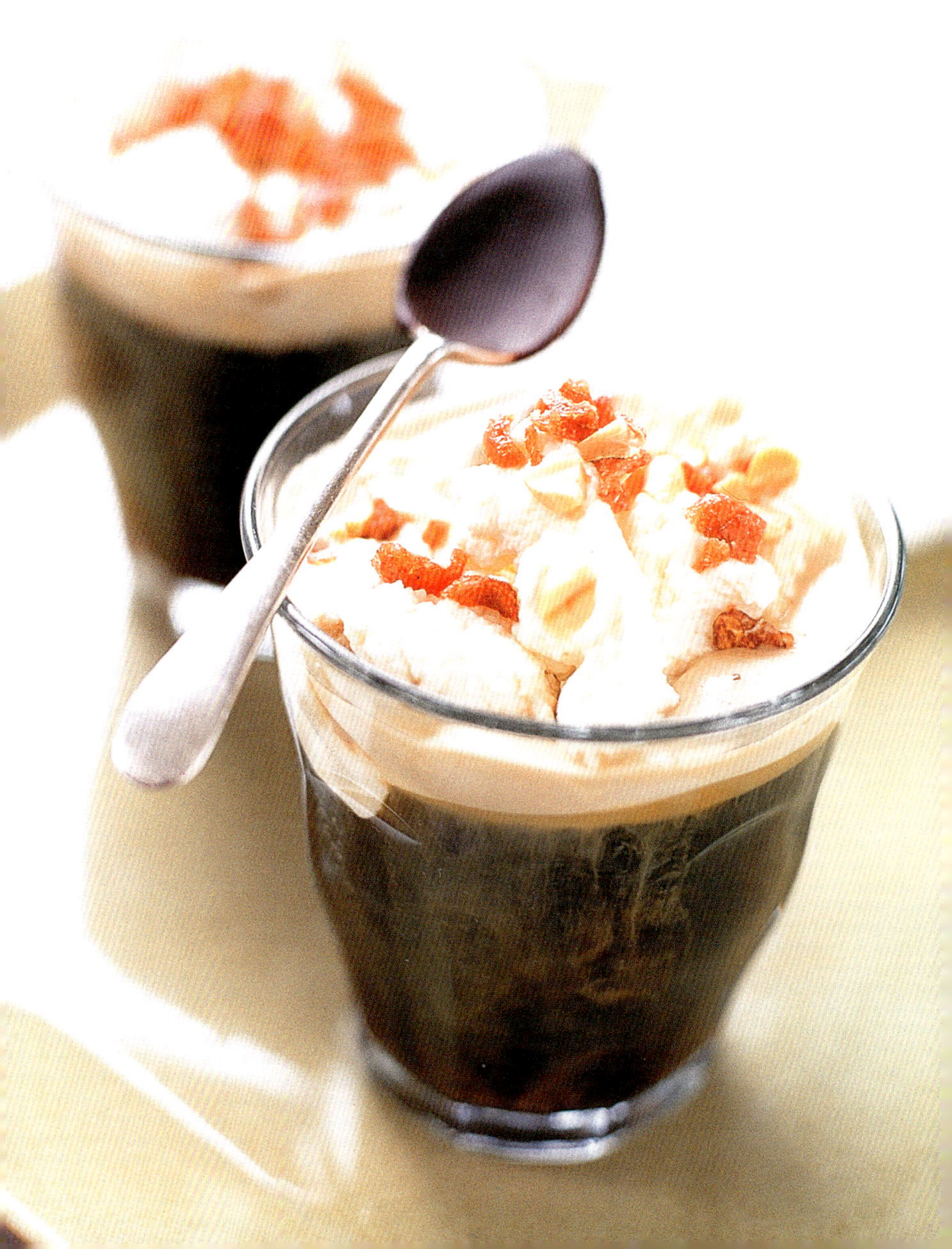

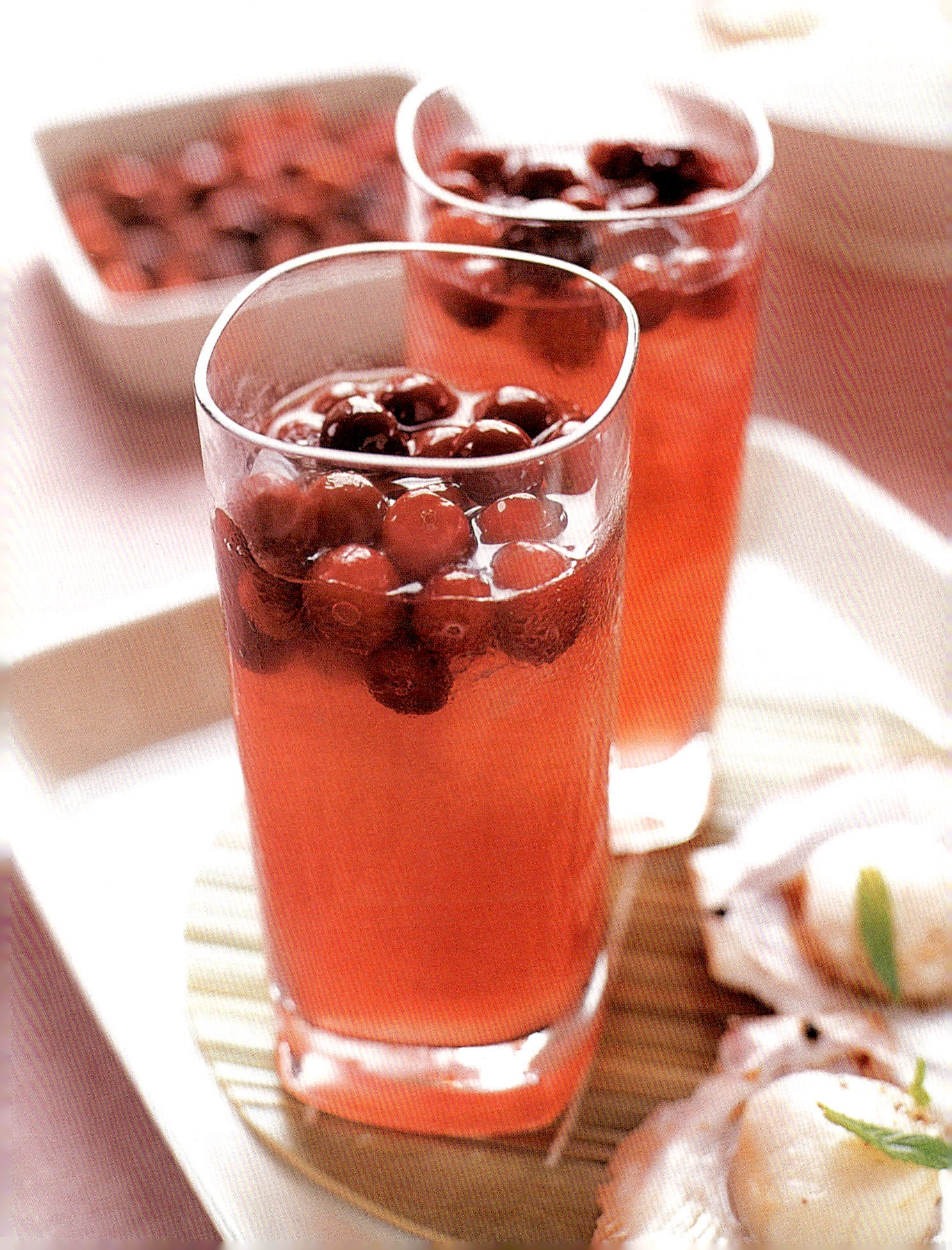

This is a variation on the Moscow mule—a mix of vodka and ginger ale. Take care when you bite into a cranberry—they are tart and have a tendency to bite back!

vodka, ginger and cranberry mule

Three-quarters fill 2 tall glasses with ice and add the cranberries. Divide the vodka between the glasses. Mix together the ginger beer and cranberry juice and pour over the vodka. Serve immediately.

Serves 2

crushed ice
60 g (2 oz) frozen cranberries
60 ml (2 fl oz) vodka
75 ml (2 1/2 fl oz) ginger beer
200 ml (6 1/2 fl oz) cranberry juice

drinks

Nothing gets the internal fires glowing like one of these sticky little shots. Try swapping the kahlua for baileys if you prefer something a bit creamier.

that's the shot

60 ml (2 fl oz) sambuca or butterscotch schnapps
60 ml (2 fl oz) kahlua
coffee beans

Pour the sambuca into 2 shot glasses. Pour the kahlua onto the sambuca over the back of a spoon so that they form separate layers. Float a few coffee beans on top.

Serves 2

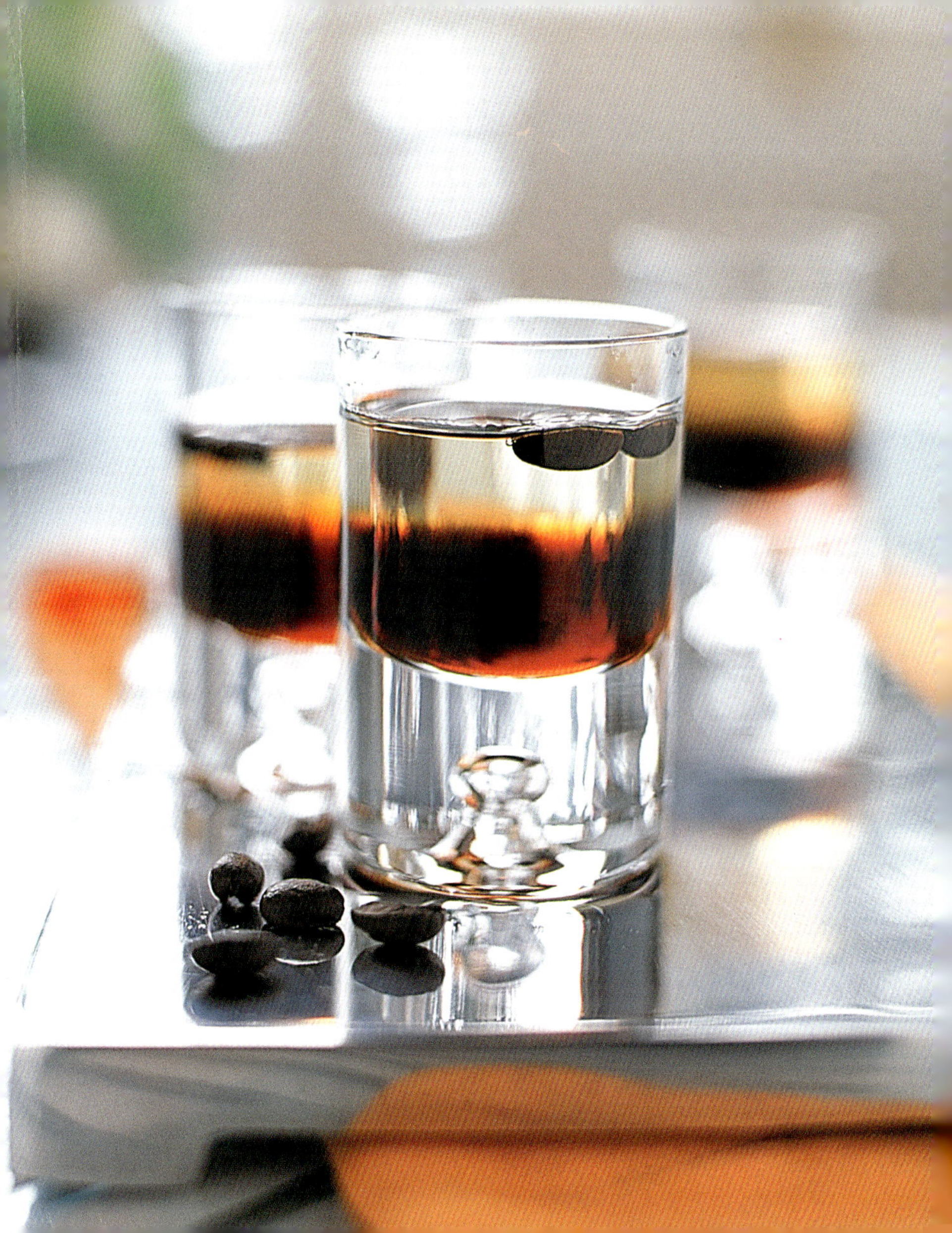

Published by Murdoch Books®, a division of Murdoch Magazines Pty Ltd,
45 Jones Street, Ultimo NSW 2007

Recipes: Jody Vassallo
Photography: Ben Dearnley
Stylist: Kristen Anderson
Food Stylist's Assistant: Michaela Le Compte
Concept and Design: Marylouise Brammer
Project Manager: Anna Waddington
Editor: Jane Price
Recipe Testing: Michaela Le Compte, Tracey Meharg

CEO & Publisher: Anne Wilson
Associate Publisher: Catie Ziller
General Manager: Mark Smith
International Sales Director: Mark Newman
Marketing Manager: Beth Drumm
National Sales Manager (News Trade): Claire Connolly
Key Accounts Manager: Luke Elworthy

National Library of Australia Cataloguing-in-Publication Data
Vassallo, Jody.
Drinks.
Includes index
ISBN 0 86411 901 1.
1. Beverages. 2. Cocktails. I. Title II. Title: Marie Claire (North Sydney, NSW).
641.87

Printed by Paramount. First printed 1999.
PRINTED IN HONG KONG.
© Text, design and photography Murdoch Books® 1999.
All rights reserved. No part of this publication may be reproduced, stored in any retrieval system or transmitted in any form or by any means, electronic, mechanical, photocopying, recording or otherwise without the prior written permission of the publisher.
Murdoch Books® is a trademark of Murdoch Magazines Pty Ltd.